# The Tuatara

## Brian Parkinson

REED

To Irene Petrov and
her Hauturu 'toots'.

Published by Reed Children's Books, an imprint of Reed
Publishing (NZ) Ltd, 39 Rawene Road, Birkenhead,
Auckland. Associated companies, branches and
representatives throughout the world.
Website: www.reed.co.nz

ISBN 1 86948 831 8
First published 2000
Reprinted 2002

Title page photograph: Henry, who is over 100 years old,
is resident at The Tuatarium, Invercargill. (L. Hazley)
Contents page: Adult tuatara. (R. Morris)
Page 14: Tuatara eating a prion egg. (R. Morris)

Edited by Carolyn Lagahetau
Designed by Sharon Whitaker

Printed in New Zealand

# Contents

# INTRODUCTION

When the supercontinent of Gondwanaland began to split apart around 120 million years ago, one of the fragments contained the beginnings of the island landmass that has become New Zealand. This slow-moving raft was very different in shape and character to the New Zealand we know today. It was not merely a piece of 'carved off' land; it was a living raft, complete with plants and animals.

With millions of years in which to develop and change, we should not be too surprised that many of the plants and animals evolved as unique species. There are some very ancient orders of animals still to be found among the survivors. Cockroaches and ferns look very much like those that first set out on this great journey.

Among the survivors of these travellers,

H. LEUE

4

R. MORRIS

there is one in particular that puzzled Victorian scientists and naturalists — the tuatara.

The tuatara has become an icon of New Zealand. This remarkable animal is the only surviving example of an ancient order of reptiles which first developed over 200 million years ago. As such it is of great interest to both the general public and the scientific community and has earned the title 'living fossil'.

Not all scientists are happy with this title as it suggests something out of date and no longer relevant. They point out that the tuatara has survived perfectly well for millions of years and, presumably, if humans had never come to New Zealand, would have continued doing so for millions more. However, the arrival of humans has thrown disorder into the development of New Zealand's plants and animals.

When the first naturalists arrived from Europe and Britain they missed the significance of these ancient-looking reptiles, thinking they were lizards, considering them curiosities but not truly remarkable. It was an understandable error, as the tuatara is similar to the Agamid lizards, which are iguanas that come from South America and the Galapagos Islands.

The incorrect placement of the tuatara with the Agamids continued for some years. On first examination the body proportions and physical features such as the well-developed head and the back crest of the tuatara made them similar to a number of types of lizards. When the first tuatara bone, a skull, arrived in Britain around 1831, John Gray of the British Museum identified it as a member of the Agamid lizards, giving it the Latin name *Sphenodon*, which means 'wedge tooth'. This name was applied because of the chisel-like teeth marks made by the upper jaw. In 1840, when Gray received a complete tuatara skeleton, he failed to recognise it as coming from the same animal. He named the 'new' reptile *Hatteria punctata*, and again called it an Agamid lizard.

In 1843, Dr Richard Owen, a scientist who studied the fossils of plants and animals (palaeontologist) at the British Museum, re-examined the remains and realised that they had striking similarities to fossil remains from South Africa. Although Owen worked at the same museum as Gray, he was unaware of Gray's description and renamed the tuatara *Rhynchocephalus*.

This mistake continued for over twenty years. It wasn't until 1867 that Dr Gunther, John Gray's successor at the British Museum, realised that *Hatteria* and *Rhynchocephalus* were one and the same animal, and that the animal was certainly no lizard. Certain physical features of the tuatara were bird- and turtle-like and others were crocodile-like. The absence of earholes and copulatory organs are features unique to the tuatara.  As a consequence of

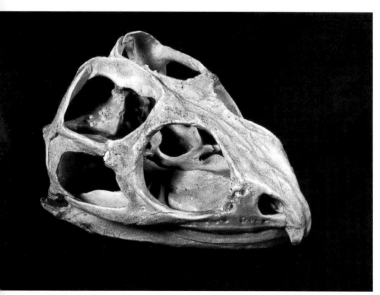

L. Hazley

*Skull of a tuatara.*

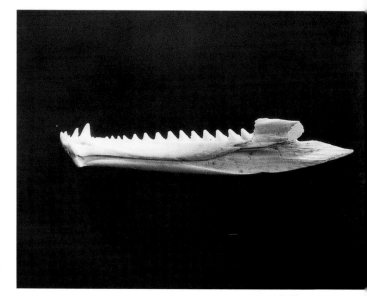

L. Hazley

*Jawbone of a tuatara.*

*Tuatara on Stephens Island, in the Marlborough Sounds.*

after all its relatives were overtaken, and probably eliminated, by more modern reptiles. The last known overseas relatives of the tuatara died out around 50 million years ago.

Until recently it was thought that there was only one species of tuatara. By using DNA studies, Dr Charles Daugherty, Professor of Ecology at Victoria University, has shown there are actually two species: *Sphenodon punctatus* and the much less common *Sphenodon guntheri*.

The fact that there are only a small number of tuatara has given the task of preserving this important animal new urgency and focus.

these differences, Dr Gunther proposed a new order for the tuatara and its fossil relatives, the *Rhynchocephalia*, which means 'beak head'. It refers to the way the upper jaw projects over the lower, a feature more noticeable in the tuatara's extinct relatives than in the tuatara itself.

One of the most interesting facts about the tuatara is that it has survived in New Zealand

*Male tuatara.*

R. MORRIS

The name tuatara is a Maori word and means 'spiny back', or 'peaks on the back'. The mana associated with tuatara is reinforced by the number of stories and proverbs about the animal found in Maori myth and legend. Tuatara and lizards are very special to Maoridom in that they represent ariki, that is, they are considered to be God forms.

However, this mana did not give the tuatara total protection; it was also eaten by Maori. Certain rituals needed to be observed when the animals were being collected; for example, people who remained behind in the village refrained from eating during the period of collection. They believed that if they did eat, the tuatara would become angry and attack the hunters. Women never ate tuatara as they are 'life-givers', like the Gods. Putting the two together would result in much turmoil! In some areas ancient Maori regarded the tuatara with awe and saw it as the messenger of Whiro, who is the spirit of death and disaster.

According to Maori legend, tuatara and lizards are children of Punga, the God of all things ugly, who once lived in the sea. The story goes that the tuatara tired of their marine existence and decided to move ashore. However, before they moved they debated with various sea creatures about the best place to live — the land or the sea. One legend from Ngati Porou of the East Coast tells of the argument between the tuatara and the shark about the best place to live.

'Greetings,' said Mango the shark. 'Come with me and let us both live in the sea.'

'No,' replied the tuatara. 'The land is the best place for me.'

'Come on, be reasonable. The sea is the place for both of us,' said the shark. At that the two began to quarrel.

'If you go to the land with your ridiculous appearance you will become the object of human disgust,' sneered the shark.

'Sure, that is my mana,' said the tuatara, 'and it will also prove to be my salvation. But you, if you go to the sea, you will be hauled out. Your mouth will be torn with a hook. You will be thrown into the bottom of the canoe and your head will be clubbed and broken with a fern root beater. And then you will be hung up to dry in the sun like a rag.'

The two separated and went their different ways;
it came to pass that their predictions came true!

J.L. Kendrick (DoC)

*A male tuatara at the entrance to his burrow.*

9

# The life cycle of the tuatara

L. HAZLEY

*A male tuatara basking in a shaft of sunlight.*

Finding a good breeding site is essential but difficult for tuatara. The forest floor is usually too cold so they look for open ground on the forest edge. On Stephens Island pasture provides conditions that the tuatara like, however, sheep become a threat when they trample the burrows tuatara live in.

The tuatara is mainly nocturnal and copes with cold temperatures by varying its body heat. By preference, it lives in much cooler conditions than lizards or snakes of equivalent size. Adults are, on the whole, slow moving, but hatchlings move quite rapidly and are considered to be at least as fast moving as lizards of a similar size. Hatchlings need to be quick on their feet, as adults are not beyond snacking on them if their paths cross. This is probably why hatchlings are diurnal and arboreal.

During hibernation, the tuatara's heart rate becomes slow and irregular, sometimes dropping as low as one beat a minute. At times, it can also slow its metabolism to a stage where several minutes will pass between each breath. On the other hand, at higher temperatures, body reactions speed up and the heart rate rises to above 30 beats per minute. Food taken at night, when it is too cold for digestion, is better processed in warmer daytime temperatures. For that reason tuatara will come out to bask in the sun during the day but will disappear back down their burrows at the first hint of danger.

*A male tuatara in mating display.*

*Tuatara often share burrows with birds such as this prion.*

M. EAGLE

*Tuatara mating.*

Tuatara take up to twenty years to reach sexual maturity. Many adults live for a very long time, but reports of individuals several hundred years old remain unproven.

On its island homes, although quite capable of digging its own burrow, the tuatara often shares tunnels dug by seabirds such as fairy prions, fluttering shearwaters, sooty shearwaters and flesh-footed shearwaters. The tuatara is not an ideal lodger as it has been known to eat or evict its roommates, or at least eggs and chicks, so it is doubtful that seabirds gain anything from this arrangement.

Although the females are relatively peaceful

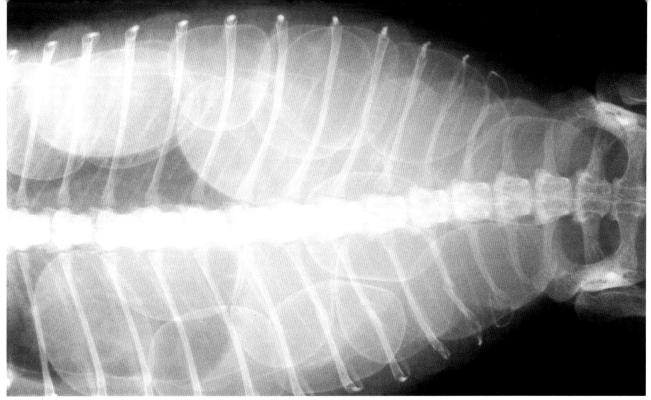

*An x-ray showing eggs in a female tuatara.*

towards one another, for the male the task of attracting a mate and driving away competing suitors is a very serious one. Courting males have been observed travelling long distances to fight. Such fights, when they do occur, follow a set ritual and include puffing up the throat sac, erecting spines, croaking and lunging. Although tuatara have sharp claws, it is their jaws that inflict the most damage during fights, and most older males carry scars from these violent encounters.

The female chooses the male, so it is the male who must display to attract her attention. He does this by standing as tall as possible outside his burrow, with his body lifted clear off the ground, his neck puffed out and spines erect. When a female approaches he circles her, walking with a peculiar stiff-legged gait called a 'stolzer gong'. If she is sufficiently impressed, she will allow mating to take place. Since the male has no penis or copulatory organ, mating begins when the male aggressively bites the female on the neck. He often turns her over, wrapping his tail around her. If they are positioned correctly, sperm flows from the male into the female's cloaca. Fertilisation usually takes place somewhere between the months of February and March.

The female's nesting period is October and November, although some eggs are not laid until December or January. She is quite secretive about egg laying, and will take her time scouting out a suitable location. Once a spot is found, she digs an underground hollow about twenty centimetres deep and one-and-a-half metres long. This can take several nights.

*Tuatara hatchlings emerging from their egg cluster.*

When excavating her nesting hole the female uses her front legs for digging and tosses the earth far behind her, like a dog burying a bone; other females in the area calmly endure these showers of dirt. The female will lay between eight and thirteen eggs in the hole.

Nesting females show scant regard for the nests of other tuatara and they will often dig over the site of another's brood. The inevitable result is exposed or broken eggs, and the consequent loss of potential hatchlings. The underground incubation of the parchment-like eggs takes from twelve to fourteen months.

Although the eggs are white when newly laid, they soon become stained with earth. As the time for hatching draws near, the egg starts to absorb moisture from the soil and the covering becomes swollen to bursting point. The tiny tuatara hatchling slits the casing with the horny egg-breaker, or caruncle, on the tip of its nose. The earth-coloured baby now faces the task of tunnelling out of the burrow. It does this by corkscrewing up through the soil until it breaks through the surface. The egg sac is still attached to the hatchling at this stage, but it soon dries up and drops off a few days later.

As soon as they reach the surface hatchlings seek cover under nearby rocks and logs. They have a number of immediate problems to contend with, such as the need to avoid drying out, overheating, and attacks from other tuatara.

Another significant problem is cannibalism, including being eaten by their own parents! This lasts until they are big enough to fend for themselves. Hatchlings are also known to seek cover by climbing trees.

Nowadays, with the added pressure of introduced predators, the risks to the hatchlings are enormous. On at least one island in the Bay of Plenty there are only adults, as juveniles no longer survive.

R. MORRIS

*Adult tuatara in kawakawa tree, Stephens Island.*

**17**

# WHERE TUATARA LIVE

*Tuatara on one of the Poor Knights Islands.*

The tuatara was once widely spread throughout the North, South and Stewart Islands of New Zealand. The evidence for this is provided by fossil remains that have been found in many parts of the country and in many geographical features such as sand dunes, peat bogs, caves and Maori middens.

Although there is some argument over why and when the tuatara disappeared from the main islands of New Zealand, the most serious factor in the decline of the North Island and northern South Island populations was most likely the kiore (Pacific rat), which arrived in New Zealand with Maori. Although adult tuatara would have been too large for kiore to attack, juveniles and eggs would have been easy prey for these rodents.

The tuatara of Southland and Stewart Island probably disappeared because the climate cooled with the last ice age. This would explain why the subfossils that have been found in these regions are much older than those found in the north. By the time Euro-peans arrived, tuatara were largely confined to offshore islands. Any remaining mainland animals were rapidly exterminated by pigs and other preda-tors that had been imported, accidentally or otherwise, by Europeans.

These small island populations were put under pressure as, one by one, the predators reached them. The tuatara of East Island, which is off the East Cape of the North Island, has been wiped out. Because of its greenish colouration and stockier build, the tuatara on this island was considered a distinct sub-species, or possibly another population of the rare Brother's tuatara. However, the population was destroyed by the kiore in the early twentieth century.

The tuatara of Whenuakura Island (near Whangamata) were also wiped out when the Norway rat reached the island as recently as the early 1980s. Other islands from which the tuatara has disappeared within living memory are the Mokohinau Islands, Slipper, Shoe, Motiti, Motuhora (Whale) and Somes Islands. Most of these extinctions were caused by rats.

In 1877, A.K. Newman wrote that 'Tuatara … [are] now only found on the off-shore islands, the pigs having eaten them on the mainland.' Dr Gunther expanded on this, recording from information that he had been given that tuatara were under threat. He noted that 'narrowly restricted in its distribution, exposed to easy capture by its sluggish habits, esteemed as food by the natives, pursued by pigs, it is one of the rarest objects in zoological and anatomical collections, and may one day be enumerated among the forms to have become extinct within the memory of man'.

In 1895, and somewhat dishonestly in light of his own collecting activities, Sir Walter Buller noted the problem of over-collection by travelling natural biologists. Buller claimed that one collector had forwarded 300 specimens, which were preserved in spirits, to Europe at one time.

Today, tuatara survive on about 30 islands which range from the Poor Knights Islands off Northland, down through the Hauraki Gulf and the Bay of Plenty to Cook Strait. Several of these island populations are a cause for alarm as their numbers are critically low. Those on Cuvier, Stanley, Red Mercury and Little Barrier Islands have required active management in order to prevent their extinction.

## The vanishing tuatara

Islands from which tuatara are known to have become extinct since the arrival of Europeans:

East Island
Mokohinau Islands
Motiti Island
Shoe Island
Slipper Island
Somes Island
Motuhora (Whale) Island
Whenuakura Island

Although no fossil evidence has been found so far, tuatara are believed to have vanished from the following islands within this period:

Chetwodes group
Great Barrier Island
Hauturu Island
Mana Island
Mayor Island islets
Moturoa Island (off Karikari Peninsula in the Far North)

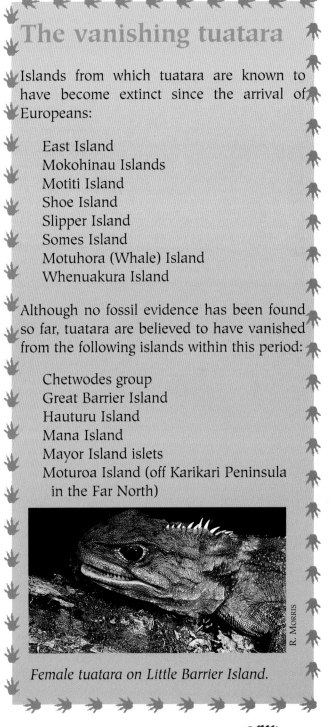

*Female tuatara on Little Barrier Island.*

R. MORRIS

# What makes tuatara different

P. Morrison (DoC)

*Tuatara with a forked tail. This is a result of regeneration.*

There are four orders of reptiles on earth today: Crocodilia, Squamata (lizards and snakes), Testudines (tortoises, turtles and terrapins), and Sphenodontida. The Sphenodontida, or 'beak-heads', of which the two tuatara species are now the only living representatives, was much more significant in the past and was thought at one time to be the dominant reptilian group during the age of the dinosaurs.

Certain physical features of the tuatara place it apart from all other reptiles and make it deserving of its own order. Among these are features shared with birds and a few fossil reptiles, for example the so-called uncinate processes. These are the hook-like structures which attach their ribs to their muscles. The skull is more robust than that found in lizards and is closer to those of the crocodile whose parts are joined by bars of bones. Other features that set the tuatara apart from lizards are the egg-tooth on the jaws of the young which enable them to break out of their shells, and the absence of earholes and copulatory organs.

# Types of tuatara

For many years it was generally considered that there was only one species of tuatara, *Sphenodon punctatus*, and that this group was divided into a number of subspecies. Current genetic research indicates there are two species and one of these is divided into two subspecies.

- Northern tuatara (*Sphenodon punctatus*)
  – Cook Strait tuatara
  – An as yet unnamed subspecies
- Brother's tuatara (*Sphenodon guntheri*)

The Little Barrier tuatara was once considered to be a separate subspecies, *Sphenodon punctatus reischeki*, but recent studies show it to be the same as tuatara on nearby islands.

*Brother's tuatara.*

In particular, one feature has caused much discussion among scientists. This is the third or parietal eye, situated on the top of the brain. The tuatara shares this characteristic with many fossil vertebrates as well as numerous modern lizards. The significance for those studying the tuatara is that in no other animal is the third eye so well-developed. This eye is visible in newborn tuatara, but as the animal grows it rapidly becomes covered in scales. This third eye has been proven to be light sensitive and, although effectively sightless, it has a rudimentary lens and retina and operates via a chemical connection to the brain. It also appears to be associated in some way with the pineal gland, and there is one current theory that ultraviolet light stimulates the pineal gland to help in early development of the tuatara. Another theory is that it acts as a more generalised biological clock.

*Pineal or third eye in a newly hatched tuatara.*

# WHO EATS WHAT

R. MORRIS

## What tuatara eat

**Earthworms**
**Insects**
**Isopods**
**Lizards**
**Seabird eggs and chicks**
**Snails**
**Spiders**

## What eats tuatara

**Adzebill***
**Black-backed gulls**
**Harriers**
**Kingfishers**
**Kiore**
**Laughing owl***
**Morepork**
**New Zealand crow***
**New Zealand goshawk***
**Norway rats**
**Ship's rats**

* extinct

R. MORRIS (DoC)

22

# A VANISHING SPECIES: SAVING THE TUATARA

Tuatara are a recognised threatened species, yet from fossil evidence it seems that at one time there were millions of tuatara on many parts of New Zealand. They were widespread and found in a range of habitats. They now occupy around 0.5 percent of their former range and are confined to a number of relatively inaccessible offshore islands. However, even in remote areas they are still in danger. Populations on at least ten of the 40 islands where they were found a hundred years ago have disappeared. From the millions of animals once evident, the population has crashed to around 100,000. Of particular concern is the plight of the Brother's tuatara, which has only about 400 surviving animals.

R. Morris (DoC)

*Juvenile tuatara, about six or seven years old.*

*Chewed and bandaged fingers and hands show that this tuatara moved a bit faster than expected!*

Recent and current museum and university studies are investigating ways of increasing the breeding success of tuatara. However, such studies are often filled with difficulty. First, it is necessary to find and catch tuatara. Since the main populations are on relatively inaccessible islands, often protected by inhospitable sheer cliffs and surrounded by frequently rough seas, even when the necessary permission has been obtained, an enthusiasm and a love for the rugged outdoors are essential for the scientist. The long lifespan and infrequent breeding cycle of the tuatara also make population studies difficult. Even when tuatara have been located, they tend to stay in their burrows during daylight hours, being nocturnal, or they quickly retreat when disturbed.

Chewed and bandaged fingers are the mark of the tuatara scientist. Tuatara prefer to live in the burrows of seabirds such as petrels and shearwaters, all of whom share the tuatara's dislike of an intruding hand. Tuatara may do most things slowly but when they bite they do so very quickly and do not willingly let go.

Some scientists have learnt their lesson and now extract tuatara from their burrows by attaching a tennis ball to the end of a plastic rod and drawing the animal out when they feel its toothed beak firmly attached to the ball. Also of concern to the researcher is the need to avoid crashing through the surface into the honeycomb of seabird burrows that are the tuatara's natural habitat. Additionally, large stinging centipedes are quite common on the islands of the Hauraki Gulf and Bay of Plenty where tuatara occur; a nip from one of these is guaranteed to make one's trip memorable.

Studies have found that islands used by smaller seabirds as nesting sites are favoured areas of tuatara. The kiore, and to a lesser extent the Norway and the Ship's rats, are a major threat to these breeding grounds, both with their destructive effect on the bird population on which the tuatara depends, and the increased competition for food they provide with their presence. Many favoured foods of the tuatara, such as ground invertebrates, lizards and smaller seabirds, are also preferred by kiore. The rats are prolific breeders and seriously diminish food available to tuatara. Kiore

*Female tuatara.*

R. Morris

*This tuatara has been fitted with a radio transmitter so its movements can be followed.*

D.G. Newman (DoC)

also prey on tuatara eggs and juveniles.

To make the study of tuatara movements more efficient, some of the animals have been fitted with small radio transmitters, which are monitored with radio tracking devices. On the Poor Knights and some other islands, researchers were at one time cutting off particular toes of tuatara to make later identification of individual animals easier. This method of identification was abandoned many years ago.

### Motuhora Island

Innovative methods have been invented to avoid further reduction in tuatara populations. New Zealand leads the world in rat and feral cat eradication from islands, and those islands that have been cleared of these pests can then be restocked with tuatara. Motuhora, or Whale Island, near Whakatane, is among the most recent islands to be restocked. Tuatara from the nearby Raurimu Rocks were transferred to Motuhora after cats and rats were exterminated.

## Red Mercury Island

In 1991, in a last attempt to save the tuatara of Red Mercury Island which were being heavily preyed on by kiore, the six remaining adults were trapped and removed to Auckland Zoo. While the kiore were being poisoned, a breeding programme for the adults was set up at the zoo, with juveniles being sent to the Otorohanga Kiwi House for raising. In 1997 six adults, along with twelve thriving juveniles, were returned to Red Mercury Island. They were welcomed back to their home by a party of local Maori.

## Cuvier Island and Somes Island

After the success of their Red Mercury Island breeding programme, the Auckland Zoo has also begun a breeding programme for tuatara off Cuvier Island, another threatened population. Additionally, a group of the much rarer Brother's tuatara was moved to Somes Island in Wellington Harbour after the island was cleared of predators. Another group has been established on an island in the Marlborough Sounds, the location of which is being kept secret by the Department of Conservation in order to avoid possible targeting by smugglers.

C.R. VEITCH (DoC)

*Tuatara on Cuvier Island.*

L. HAZLEY

*The Tuatarium at the Southland Art Gallery and Museum, Invercargill.*

### Little Barrier Island

The future for the few remaining tuatara of the Little Barrier Island population is now also looking considerably brighter. In an effort to protect them from kiore which still infest the area, eight of the remaining adults have been brought together in a managed colony on the island. As eggs are laid they are sent to Victoria University for incubation. The juveniles are returned to the colony when they are thought to be big enough to fend for themselves.

A programme for eradicating the kiore is planned. When this is completed the tuatara colony can be released to begin repopulation of the island. A conservative estimate is that the island could support an eventual population of several hundred thousand tuatara. If this is achieved the future for this reptile would be a lot brighter.

### The Tuatarium, Invercargill

Breeding techniques have improved considerably since initial bumpy starts. The Tuatarium at Invercargill has long been a leader in this field, having recently achieved a world first when a second generation female laid eggs at the facility.

# SMUGGLING

In the past tuatara have been advertised in the United States for as much as US$10,000 each; there has also been one mail order firm advertising tuatara skulls for sale. As only a few export permits for tuatara have ever been granted to zoos in Europe and the United States, these cases are proof that there is illegal export of these animals.

It is well known that tuatara are highly sought after by reptile collectors in both North America and Europe, and several attempts have been made to smuggle live animals abroad. In 1991, two tuatara were stolen from the Tuatarium at Invercargill. In 1997, tuatara stolen from Stephens Island were intercepted by Department of Conservation officers in a roadside park near Geraldine in the South Island.

The smuggling of our animals is regarded with increasing seriousness by law enforcement authorities. This concern is reflected in the severity of the sentences being handed down to offenders.

DoC, GERALDINE

DoC, Geraldine

*This tuatara was intercepted as smugglers tried to remove it from New Zealand for sale overseas.*

# GLOSSARY

| | |
|---|---|
| arboreal | relating to, or living in trees |
| burrow | a hole or a tunnel dug by a small animal to be used as a home |
| caruncle | a fleshy growth, such as a bird's wattle |
| cloaca | the cavity through which sperm enters the female tuatara |
| diurnal | of or during the daytime |
| extinct | no longer in existence |
| fertilisation | to make offspring by the joining of male and female reproductive material |
| fossil | the remains or impression of a prehistoric plant or animal |
| hatchling | a newly hatched young animal |
| hibernation | to spend the winter in an inactive state |
| incubation | to sit on eggs to keep them warm so they will hatch |
| invertebrate | an animal without a backbone or spine |
| isopod | a crustacean with a flattened body and seven pairs of legs, for example a woodlouse |
| metabolism | chemical processes in the body which encourage growth and produces energy |
| midden | a place for rubbish |
| nocturnal | to be active at night |
| pineal gland | a small growth on top of the head, in tuatara it is thought to be light-sensitive |
| reptile | a cold-blooded animal |
| tuatara | a burrowing, lizard-like reptile with a crest of soft spines |
| vertebrate | an animal with a backbone or spine |

M. BARRIBALL

# INDEX

R. Morris (DoC)